CW00376029

a gift for us to share

to: TAYLOR RAY . . . .

from: GRAMPY DAVE . . . .

X

OTHER HELEN EXLEY®LONDON BOOKS IN THIS SERIES:
Me and my Dad
Me and my Grandma
Me and my Mum

OTHER HELEN EXLEY® LONDON BOOKS:
To a very special Grandpa
To the lovliest Granddaughter
Thanks Dad!

ISBN 978-1-78485-081-4

10 9   8   7   6   5   4   3   2   1

Copyright © Helen Exley Creative Ltd 2016
Illustrations © Jane Massey 2005, 2015, 2016
Design, selection, arrangement and words are all
© Helen Exley Creative Ltd 2016
Published in 2016 by Helen Exley ®
LONDON in Great Britain.

The moral right of the author has been asserted.
A copy of the CIP data is available from the British Library
on request. All rights reserved. No part of this publication
may be reproduced or transmitted in any form or by any
means without permission in writing from the publisher.

Printed in Turkey.

Helen Exley Gifts,
16 Chalk Hill, Watford,
Herts WD19 4BG, UK.
www.helenexley.com

Me
and my
Grandad

Written by Helen Exley and Illustrated by Jane Massey

I love my Grandad.

And I love it most

when I stay with him.

He always waits by the window

for me to arrive.

when I stay at Grandad's
he always has a special look
in his eye, and a kind of soft smile.
I help him build things in his workshop.
we eat chocolate bars that he buys
specially for me. Usually he forgets
they're for me and eats most
of them himself.

My Grandad often shows me
his family photos.
He's proud of his children
and his grandchildren.
Especially me.

Grandad marks pages in his books to read with me. Did you know that he keeps hundreds and hundreds of his old books just to share with me?

One night I woke up terribly scared because a bad bear was after me. Grandad chased the scariness away. He always does. He protects me like this, and makes me feel safe.

Grandad and I often play cards together. I used to think he was a bit slow, because he always lost. But then I discovered he was letting me win because he was being kind.

Grandad tells me that he used to do rough and tumble things with my Dad. But now it seems they're both past it. Grandad's still quite strong, though. When he took me golfing, one shot broke the clubhouse window.

Grandad's good fun, and he's game for almost anything. But he turns a bit green on round-a-bouts and swings, so then I have to look after him.

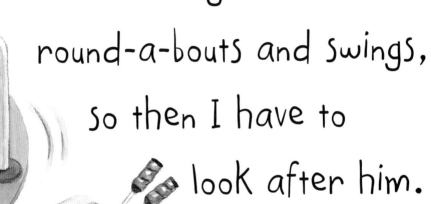

I write to my Grandad and tell him all the news. He writes back to me. It used to be to help me to learn to read but now it stops us both from being lonely.

My Grandad always, always carries my letters in his briefcase when he goes to work.

He reads them and looks at all the photos of our family.

And of me.

Grandad and I just play
and play, and talk and talk.
But then Grandad gets tired
and goes to sleep.
Then it's my turn to watch
out for him, so I have
to keep very QUIET.

Do you know that every year Grandad grows strawberries just for me? How can I ever say "Thank you" for the strawberries and the chocolates and the hugs and letters?

There are no words that
can ever say "Thank you" big enough!

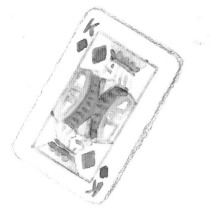

WHAT IS A HELEN EXLEY GIFTBOOK?

Helen Exley has been creating Gift Books for forty years,
and her readers have bought more than 141 million copies
of her works in forty five languages.

Because her books are bought as gifts, she makes sure
that each book is as thoughtful and meaningful a gift
as it is possible to create: good to give, good to receive.

You have the result in your hands.
If you have found it valuable - tell others!